One Careful Owner

A Play

H. Connolly

A Samuel French Acting Edition

SAMUEL FRENCH

FOUNDED 1830

SAMUELFRENCH-LONDON.CO.UK
SAMUELFRENCH.COM

ISBN 978-0-573-12160-9

www.samuelfrench-london.co.uk

www.samuelfrench.com

FOR AMATEUR PRODUCTION ENQUIRIES

UNITED KINGDOM AND WORLD
EXCLUDING NORTH AMERICA
plays@SamuelFrench-London.co.uk
020 7255 4302/01

Each title is subject to availability from Samuel French,

depending upon country of performance.

CHARACTERS

Darren, late 20s
Percival, aged 55
Jane, late 20s
Tony, late 20s

The action takes place in Darren's front room

Time — the present

ONE CAREFUL OWNER

The front room of a working-class house

There is a door DSR *to the hall and front door, another door* DSL *to the kitchen and a window* USC

There is a cabinet USL, *a cottage-style sofa and an armchair with a coffee table between them* DSR. *There is a wedding photo on the table and a gong on the cabinet.* USR *is a plant stand. The sofa is covered in empty crisp packets, old newspapers and sweet wrappings. On the armchair is a pile of washing waiting to be ironed*

As the CURTAIN *rises Darren walks in from the kitchen. He carries two mugs of coffee. On the way to the table, he looks out of the window*

Darren Come on, for God's sake. You either want it or you don't. (*He walks with the mugs to the table*) It's only a second-hand car you're buying, not a thoroughbred racehorse. (*He puts the cups on the table*) It's a wonder he doesn't start shoving his arm up the bloody exhaust pipe. (*He sits on the sofa*) I suppose he'll try and knock me down in price. I don't know how he'll have the nerve to. I mean how can he argue about the price of a Citroen 2CV when he comes to look at it in a brand new Rolls Royce? (*He thinks to himself and smiles*) Maybe he wants to do a swap? (*He stops smiling*) I've just thought — maybe he's a tax inspector! (*He drinks his coffee slowly. He takes one foot out of his slipper and puts it on the coffee table. His big toe is poking through a hole in his sock. He talks to his toe*) Do you hear that, Pinky? It might be the tax man. (*He points to the door with his thumb, then he takes*

*his other foot out of the slipper, and puts it on the table. A big toe
sticks out of this sock too*) Yes, Perky. Yes, I know you and your
brother have never filled in a tax return, but that's no excuse.
They've caught up with you at last and they want their pound of
flesh. (*Both feet dive under the table*) All right! All right! I'm
sorry. (*He slowly puts both feet back on the table*) It wasn't a very
clever thing to say about two pigs.

The front doorbell rings

Don't worry, boys, if it's the tax man I'll get you the same lawyer
as Ken Dodd had. (*He stands up, puts his mug on the table and
puts his slippers back on. He realizes what he has just been doing*)
I'm spending too much time on my own. I've got to get out and
talk to real people.

The doorbell rings again. He goes to answer it

(*Off*) Please go through. I've made you coffee.
Percival (*off*) Thank you. That's very kind of you.

*Percival walks in. He is in his middle fifties, well dressed in an
expensive suit and coat. He carries his bowler hat. Darren enters*

Darren Would you like to sit down. (*He points to the sofa*)
Percival (*looking at the sofa*) Well, I don't know.

Darren quickly throws everything from the sofa underneath it

Darren Let me take your coat.
Percival Yes. It is quite expensive.

*He gives Darren his hat and takes off his coat. Darren carefully
folds the coat up. Percival picks up a blackened banana skin from
the corner of the sofa, and holds it up. Darren throws Percival's
coat and hat on the sofa, takes the banana skin and throws it under
the sofa. Percival sits at the other end of the sofa*

Darren I've given you a mug. I hope that's OK.
Percival (*holding the mug up*) How quaint.

Darren sits in the armchair, jumps up again, throws the washing under the armchair and sits down again. Percival takes a sip of his coffee — he doesn't like it

Darren What do you think of her?
Percival Whom? (*He puts his mug down*)
Darren The car.
Percival Oh yes.
Darren She's a beauty, ain't she? As good as new if not better after the work I've done on her.
Percival Your work includes the garter hanging over the rear-view mirror, does it?
Darren Well, that's just to give her a bit of character.
Percival What about the sticker?
Darren Sticker?
Percival The "I may be old and slow but I'm in front of you, you impatient bastard" sticker in the rear window.
Darren Ah, that's just a bit of fun — It's one of mine, you know. You can get them made up in a shop in the High Street.
Percival (*not interested*) Oh really?
Darren Yeah. He'll do anything you like. (*Leaning towards Percival*) Don't matter how rude. You should have seen the one I wanted first of all!
Percival A literary feast, no doubt. Tell me, whose idea was it to put transfers on both the doors?
Darren Oh, that was the wife's. I told her it was stupid. I mean, who wants to be seen driving down the road with Mr Rusty and Brian the Snail on your doors.
Percival I'm sorry?
Darren You know. *The Magic Roundabout.*
Percival No, I'm afraid not. Is it near here?
Darren No. They're characters from a kids' programme. You must have seen it.

Percival I can't say I have.

Darren It had a tomato bouncing about on a big coiled spring and he kept telling the old tart in the show it was time for bed, but she was only interested in getting off with Dylan, the work-shy, drug-taking rabbit. (*He thinks*) At least, that's how it always seemed to me.

Percival If I have the car I'm not interested in these accessories.

Darren What?

Percival The sticker, the garter and most definitely the transfers. They will have to go.

Darren Well, you've only got to take them off, ain't you? I mean, Gordon Bennett, it's not too difficult.

Percival Yes, I agree, the garter and the sticker are easy enough, but what about the transfers on the door?

Darren Well, they'll come off.

Percival But that means the paintwork on the doors will be a different shade from the rest of the car.

Darren Well, what's wrong with that?

Percival If I buy the car it will be for my wife's use and she's very fussy.

Darren I suppose you're going to try and knock off the price of a re-spray.

Percival Well, I think that would be the least I could expect.

Darren I told the silly mare it weren't a good idea.

Percival Look, I'll be honest with you.

Darren Oh God! That means I need a lawyer!

Percival (*standing*) Look, Mr Whatever-your-name-is, I'm a gentleman of my word.

Darren Trollop. (*He stands too*)

Percival (*upset*) I can assure you, Sir, I am.

Darren No. My name's Trollop. (*He shakes Percival's hand*)

Percival Oh, I'm sorry.

Darren So am I. It's been murder to live with. (*He sits*)

Percival I'm sure it must be. (*He sits too*)

Darren My Dad went to the same school as me.

Percival Well, you mustn't hold it against them. I'm sure they tried their best with both of you.

Darren He was the first Trollop to go to that school.
Percival Really?
Darren He was there before me.
Percival One would assume so if he was your father.
Darren We had nearly all the same teachers, so when I gets there they calls me "the little Trollop", don't they?
Percival Oh, right.
Darren Do you know what that can do to a man to be known all through school as "the little Trollop"?
Percival Everyone has to suffer the same at school.
Darren I bet you didn't. (*He goes to Percival*)
Percival I can assure you I did.
Darren Go on, then. What's your last name?
Percival (*reluctantly*) Hitchcock.

Darren looks at him

Darren Oh well, then. Perhaps you did. (*He walks away*) But I'd have swapped that for Trollop in an instant. (*He thinks again*) What did the kids call you at school?
Percival (*too quickly*) I can't remember.
Darren Go on. You must have had a nickname.
Percival It's of no importance.
Darren Let me see if I can guess. (*He walks around the sofa thinking*) Hitchcock — Hitchcock ——
Percival Really. It doesn't matter.
Darren (*splitting the name up*) Hitch — cock — Hitch — cock —
Percival Please. This is silly.
Darren Hitch — cock. (*He has an idea*) I know what your nickname was!
Percival What?
Darren I bet they called you "Drawback Dick", didn't they?
Percival I beg your pardon?
Darren Don't you get it? Hitch is the drawback and ——
Percival Yes. I can follow your reasoning but you're wrong.
Darren Well, what did they call you, then?
Percival If you must know, it was Alfred.

Darren Alfred. (*He thinks*) Alfred. No, that's lost on me. (*He sits in the chair*)

Percival As in Alfred Hitchcock, the film director.

Darren Oh, right. (*Not very impressed*) The finest public school education money can buy and that's the best they can come up with.

Percival So you're not the only one that had to suffer.

Darren That's not suffering. Alfred I can live with.

Percival Look, Mr Trollop.

Darren Please call me by my first name.

Percival Very well. What is it?

Darren Darren. Call me Darren.

Percival If I must.

Darren And what shall I call you?

Percival thinks

Percival Percival.

Darren laughs

Darren Bloody Hell. Percival. (*He laughs again*) And the kids still called you Alfred at school?

Percival stands up; annoyed

Percival Now look, Mr Troll —

Darren holds his finger up

Now look, Darren!

Darren Yes, Percival. (*He sniggers again*)

Percival At school in Harrow we had five Percivals in my year alone. In fact my best friend happened to be another Percival. We were inseparable.

Darren You don't see that very often.

Percival What?

Darren Two Percys hanging out together. (*He laughs*)

Percival (*even more angry*) What I'm trying to say is that in my circle of friends at public school, Percival was a very common name and therefore not the never-ending fountain of merriment you find it to be.

Darren And Alfred was?

Percival Yes. (*He sits on the sofa again*)

Darren I'm glad I never went to your school.

Percival A statement with which I can wholeheartedly agree, Darren.

Darren I was the only Trollop at my school.

Percival (*in disbelief*) Oh no! (*He holds his head*)

Darren Unless you count my younger sister, of course.

Percival Your sister was at your school?

Darren Most of the time.

Percival Then you couldn't have been the only Trollop there, could you?

Darren I was supposed to be. It was an All Boys school.

Percival Oh my God!

Darren Now my sister, she really is a little trollop, but that's a different story.

Percival (*trying to control his anger*) Mr Troll — Darren. (*He looks up*) I'm a very busy man and I've given up a great deal of my time this morning to come and look at the car you advertised for sale in the Auto Trader. Now normally my chauffeur would sort all this out but he's on a fly-drive holiday to America —

Darren That's not much of a holiday if he's driving.

Percival (*slams the table*) Mr Trollop!

Darren Yes?

Percival Will you let me finish?

Darren Sorry.

Percival Now my wife for some inexplicable reason likes Citroen 2CVs. God knows why. Perhaps she likes the this-is-the-one-I-made-earlier look they have. But she had one before and from what I can remember it was almost identical to the one you have for sale. The same year of make, same colour, everything.

Darren Except Brian and Mr Rusty.

Percival Most definitely. Now, unfortunately she wrote her car off
in an accident.
Darren She was probably doing 35 and hit a hedgehog.
Percival Please, Mr Trollop, I've nearly finished and then we can
talk finances.
Darren Sorry — They're stronger than they look, you know.
Percival What? Citroen 2CVs?
Darren No. Hedgehogs.
Percival For the love of God! (*He jumps up*)
Darren Right. Right. I'll sit quiet.
Percival Thank you. Now — where was I?
Darren She wrote the car off.
Percival Yes. (*He sits again*) And ever since she's been on at me
about getting one to replace it. So, when I saw your advert in the
paper, and having business in this area, I thought I'd take a look
at it and, if it was suitable, buy it.
Darren And is it suitable?
Percival Apart from the transfers, yes.
Darren Oh good.
Percival There. That didn't take long, did it?

Darren stares at Percival

(*Seeing Darren staring at him*)What are you looking at?

Darren stands up

Darren I just keep thinking I've seen you some place before. (*He
looks again*) It's the telly! I've seen you on the telly.
Percival (*liking the attention*) You may have.
Darren What was it in? (*He looks again*) You're not anything to
do with Breakfast Television, are you?
Percival Please. Do I look as if I have no imagination?

Darren thinks

Darren I know! It's adverts! You do adverts, don't you?

Percival No, I don't.
Darren You can't be very famous, then. (*He sits in the chair*)
Percival If you must know, I'm an MP.
Darren (*sitting up; open-mouthed*) No! I don't believe it!

Percival smiles

You're having me on.
Percival I can assure you I'm not.
Darren Well, would you believe it! A Military Policeman with a
   Rolls Royce!

Percival jumps up

Percival I am not a Military Policeman! My name is Percival
   Hitchcock. I'm a Member of Parliament and I'm on television
   most mornings with "Westminster Today".
Darren Oh, I see.
Percival My father happened to be a Lord.
Darren Mine happened to be a drunken layabout.
Percival When I retire from politics, I shall become Lord Percival
   Hitchcock the Second.
Darren Oh God! A lord-in-waiting and I've gone and given you a
   mug!
Percival I shall inherit his title and his seat in the House of Lords.
Darren All I got was my old man's seat on the dominoes table at
   the *Frog and Firkin*.
Percival There's been a Hitchcock sitting in Parliament for
   generations.
Darren He's probably died of boredom and no-one's noticed.
Percival It has been known to get quite exciting at times. (*He sits
   on the sofa*)
Darren I preferred it when they had the test card. (*He thinks again*)
   Here. Which way do you hang?
Percival I beg your pardon?
Darren You know. Your political portion.

Percival thinks

Percival Oh. My political persuasion.
Darren Yeah. That's it.
Percival I'm Tory MP for Purmensey South West.
Darren I should have known of course. 'Cos you got a Roller, ain't you? I mean if you'd been a Labour MP you'd have arrived to buy a second-hand Rolls Royce in a brand new Citroen 2CV.
Percival And what if I were a Liberal Democrat?
Darren Oh, you'd have probably come up the path on a skateboard. I didn't vote for you, you know.
Percival I would hope not. I'm not your MP. My constituency is miles from here.
Darren No, I meant your lot. The Tories.
Percival So, for whom did you vote?
Darren The Green Party.
Percival Oh. How very non-committal. And what in God's name persuaded you to do that?
Darren I don't know really. I think maybe because it was my favourite colour.

Percival holds his head again

Percival And to think people die for the right to vote.
Darren My wife didn't vote for you either.
Percival That's all right because both of mine did.
Darren (*shocked*) Both of them!
Percival Yes. My wife and my ex-wife.
Darren Oh. Right. What does your wife do?
Percival Well, if you must know, she works with the homeless in London.
Darren It's nice for you both to have jobs with something in common.
Percival What do you mean?
Darren Well, your lot make them homeless then she tries to re-house them again.

Percival (*a bit upset*) Yes. I sometimes think that's how Amanda sees it too, but only because she spends so much time with the wrong sort of people.

Darren My wife works away a lot as well.

Percival (*sarcastically*) Well, you do surprise me!

Darren She's an air hostess. She works a week-about.

Percival What's a week-about?

Darren About seven days, ain't it? (*He laughs at his own joke*) I've tried to make her give it up but she loves it and anyway the money's good.

Percival How do you cope with being on your own so much.

Darren Oh, it's all right.

Percival Don't you get lonely?

Darren No. I talk to my big toe a lot. (*He takes his foot out of his slipper and shows him*)

Percival What!

Darren Not really. I'm knocking off the young widow who lives next door, ain't I? (*He puts his foot back into his slipper*)

Percival (*taken aback*) Oh. Oh, I see.

Darren Well, it's the wife's fault. I mean if she wasn't always in foreign parts then neither would I be.

Percival My wife works away a lot as well, but then I'm hardly ever at home either. You know, we have to phone each other every few days to make an appointment to meet.

Darren No!

Percival Oh yes. I don't want it to end how my first marriage did, in divorce. You see, Amanda is quite a lot younger than I am and very pretty.

Darren Me and Jane, my missus, are both near enough the same age.

Percival We have only been married a few months, you know.

Darren Very nice — I wish I had.

Percival That's why I don't mind her having her charity work. It keeps her occupied while I'm in the City all week.

Darren (*standing*) I'm an entertainer too, you know.

Percival Mr Trollop. I'm an MP. It has nothing whatsoever to do with entertainment.

Darren You want to try videoing your show sometime. That's the reason I want to change the car. I'm becoming more famous around the clubs and I don't want to be seen by my public in a Citroen 2CV. It's the wife's car really.
Percival Then why are you selling it?
Darren She doesn't know I am. She's at work.
Percival Surely you can't do that.
Darren I've made every decision for Jane since she left school. She's never been good at choosing things.
Percival (*looking at him*) Obviously not.
Darren If the truth was known, I've guided her through all her life.
Percival Wouldn't she have preferred a St. Christopher?
Darren If I sell her car now and buy us another one before she gets back from work, she'll come round to my way of thinking.
Percival What? Bi-annually?
Darren Oh, you're right. She'd buy anything.
Percival I don't know. I mean, if it's your wife's car —
Darren Believe me, it's all right. Now, I bet you don't know who I'm into.
Percival The widow next door so you told me.
Darren No. In my job as an entertainer.
Percival Oh. (*He thinks*) You're a warm-up man for "Mastermind"?
Darren No. I'll give you a clue. (*He moves* DSR, *shakes his leg and sneers*)

Percival looks on bemused

Percival (*getting up*) Could you run that past me again?

Darren shakes his leg and sneers again

You're a contestant on "One Man and his Randy Dog"?
Darren No. Look, I'll tell you what. I'll go and put some of my gear on.
Percival (*looking at his watch*) Look. Please. Really. I haven't got the time.

Darren It won't take a minute. I won't put it all on. Just enough to give you the flavour. (*He goes to the hall and turns*) You're going to love it. Some people honestly can't tell the difference.

He goes out

Percival goes to the door

Percival Please, Mr Trollop, I only want to buy the car.

We hear Darren running upstairs

(*Turning back to the sofa*) I can't believe it. (*He looks at his watch*) In less than an hour's time I've got a very important meeting with a top Cabinet Minister and here I am waiting to be entertained by a lunatic cross-dressing Madame Butterfly. (*He sits on the sofa*) Not a lot of difference, really, when you think about it. (*He looks at his watch again and crosses his legs, waiting. He has another sip of his coffee — it tastes just as bad. He looks at his watch again and gets up*) Oh really, this is too much. (*He walks around the back of the sofa, sees his coat in a heap, folds it neatly and puts his bowler on top of it. He spies the drink on the cabinet and walks over to it, looks towards the door then picks up the bottle of whisky*)

The front door slams

Percival quickly puts the bottle down and stands behind the sofa

A pretty woman walks into the room. She stands for a few seconds looking for something in her handbag

Percival looks at her but she doesn't see him

She walks past him, still searching in her handbag

Hallo, darling!

Jane (*turning and seeing him*) Oh hallo, Percival. (*She kisses him on the cheek and walks* DSL. *She stops, thinks, then looks at Percival*) Oh my God, (*looking out front*) right house, wrong man.

Percival (*shocked*) Amanda!

Jane (*turning to face him*) Percival! What are you doing here?

Percival Buying back my old car, it would seem.

As Percival says this, Darren comes barging through the door. He is dressed in his best Elvis gear, complete with wig. A "Mickey Mouse" purse hangs round his neck. He carries a guitar

Darren strums the guitar but it is obvious he cannot play a note. However, he gives it all he's got in a very bad rendition of "You ain't Nothing but a Hound Dog"

Jane watches, then puts her bag on the cabinet, walks over to Darren and grabs the guitar from him

Darren What did you do that for, Jane? You've cut me off in full flow. (*He kisses her on the cheek*) Anyway I wasn't expecting you home till Friday.

Percival stands open-mouthed

Jane places the guitar USR *against the plant stand. Darren notices Percival*

Percival I don't believe it!

Darren See? (*He holds his cape open*) I told you it would knock you out, didn't I?

Percival That's my wife!

Darren No it's not. It's Elvis. Your wife hasn't got sideburns, has she?

Percival No! (*He points to Jane*) That's my wife, Amanda. It's not her coat but it's definitely my wife inside it.

Darren No, it's not. There's been some kind of misunderstanding. (*He picks up the wedding photo from the table*) Look.

He shows Percival the photo

That's my wife Jane and that's me stood next to her on our wedding day.

Percival (*looking at the photo*) She's not your wife, she's mine. She even kissed me on her way in.

Both men turn and look at Jane

Jane I can explain this — I hope. (*She takes her coat off*)

Darren You are his wife?

Jane Yes. I'm afraid I am. (*She hangs her coat on the back of the armchair*)

Percival (*looking at the photo again*) And you're his wife as well, aren't you?

Jane Yes — sorry.

The men look at each other

Percival (*suddenly snapping*) You know what this means, don't you?

Darren Yeah. She's paying double Council Tax.

Percival No. I mean the legal consequences.

Darren It's bigamy!

Percival No, it's not.

Darren I suppose it's big-of-you then!

Percival The name's polyandry.

Darren Make up your mind. You was calling her Amanda just now.

Percival No, you idiot! When a woman is married to two men, it's called polyandry.

Darren thinks

Darren I knew that.

Percival Oh God. (*He is in a state of shock*)
Jane Why don't you sit down. I've got something to tell you both.
Darren You haven't got the sack, have you?
Jane No.
Darren Then what are you doing home early?
Percival (*he cannot believe this is happening*) I'm going to have to
    resign. I'm finished! (*He sits on the sofa*)
Jane Please, Darren. Sit down. I want to explain.
Percival This I've got to hear. I've been in politics for nearly thirty
    years. I've heard men talk their way out of seemingly impossible
    situations. But this I've got to hear.
Darren (*like he's coming out of a daze*) You can't be his wife.
Jane Yes, Darren. I'm afraid I am.
Darren But you was my wife first, weren't you? (*He holds up the
    photo*)
Jane Yes, I was. (*She takes the photo from him*)
Darren Well, that's it then. I branded you. You're mine.

*Darren sits on the sofa next to Percival who quickly pulls his bowler
hat out of the way before Darren sits on it. He can, however, do
nothing about his coat*

Jane I think we all need a drink. (*She slowly walks to the sideboard*)
Percival I don't want a drink. All I want is an explanation.
Darren I'll have his, then.

Percival puts his hat under the table

Jane I know this has come as a big shock to you both.
Darren (*still not with it*) I'll say so — I wasn't expecting you home
    till Friday.
Percival I wasn't expecting her here at all.
Jane Yes, well ... (*She gives them both a drink*)
Percival I can't damn well believe this. I'm sitting calmly having
    a drink in a stranger's house while my wife explains to me how
    she lives in it with Elvis Presley. This will make the Profumo
    affair look like the Sooty Show.

Darren Well, you politicians always like to keep your hand up something.
Percival Oh, do be quiet! (*He throws back his drink in one go, then spits most of it back*) What the hell's this? (*He holds up his glass*)
Jane Damson wine.
Percival Christ! I thought it was whisky.
Darren No. Damson wine.
Percival Well it came out of a whisky bottle.
Darren (*holding up his glass*) Home made. What do you think?
Percival I think I'm going to be ill.
Darren That good, eh?
Percival (*to Jane*) Well, come on then. Tell me how you tricked me.
Darren We didn't trick you. We always put damson wine in old whisky bottles.
Percival (*annoyed*) You're doing this on purpose, aren't you?
Darren No, I'm not. Honest. I mean, if you feel that strongly about it I've got some lager in the fridge.
Percival That's it! (*He stands*) I'm afraid you leave me no alternative. I'm going to have to take you to task. (*He holds his fists up ready to box and walks behind the sofa*)
Darren What?
Jane Please, Percival, don't start anything.
Darren Oh yeah! (*He stands*) You want a punch-up then?
Percival If you could oblige.

Darren walks behind the sofa

Darren (*putting his fists up*) Mr Tough-Guy now, are we? Just because your wife's watching!
Percival She's your wife as well, for God's sake, man!
Darren Oh. (*He thinks*) Well, you're just lucky I don't get aggressive like you after a drink.

Percival moves Jane away

Percival I'm now going to thrash you.

Darren (*moving back*) Don't get blood on my cape, it cost a fortune.

Percival moves to Darren who runs around the sofa and chair pursued by Percival

Percival Stand and fight, man.

They are back in their starting positions

Darren I will — I will — I'm just picking my moment.

They square up again. Darren moves around in a circle

Percival For God's sake, man. I've seen more backbone in a pot of caviar.

Darren runs around the sofa again but Percival runs round the other way and grabs him

Got you!

They wrestle for a while. Jane comes over and pulls Percival away

Jane Stop it! Stop it, the pair of you! This is all my fault.

Percival suddenly grabs his chest. Jane holds on to him. He is breathing hard

Percival, are you all right?
Percival (*leaning on her*) Get me to the chair.

She helps him to the armchair

Darren Ahh! You fell into my trap. Now you're knackered I'm going to whoop you.
Jane Shut up, Darren, and help me.

They help Percival in to the chair

   Is it your heart?

He nods

   Where are your tablets?
Percival In my jacket. (*He sits*)

Jane quickly goes through his pockets

Jane Get some water, Darren. Quickly!
Darren Right.

   Darren runs out to the kitchen. He takes the two mugs out on his way

Jane finds the tablets in Percival's pocket

Jane You know you shouldn't get excited like that.
Percival (*holding his chest; shouting through the pain*) Shouldn't get excited! Shouldn't get excited! You're giving me tablets for my angina while your first husband whom you forgot to divorce runs to fetch me some water and you tell me not to get excited.

   Darren comes in with the water and gives it to Jane. She hands it to Percival

Jane Here. Drink this.

Percival takes his tablets

   Are you feeling better now?
Percival As well as I'm ever going to feel again.
Jane Do you want me to continue with my explanation?
Percival Oh pray do, please. I wouldn't miss this even for death.
Jane I don't know where to start. (*She moves* DSR)

Percival "Once upon a time", most fairy stories kick off with.

Darren Or "twice upon a time" in her case.

Jane If you're both going to keep interfering, I'm never going to get through this.

Darren Oh, begging your humble pardon. We're just both your husbands, you know. That's all.

Jane Shut up, Darren. For once in your life don't open your mouth to speak just because no-one else is talking.

Darren Sorry, I'm sure. (*He sits on the end of the sofa*) Anyone would think I was the guilty party.

Jane That's it, really. You are. When I first met you I was very young and impressionable. I thought you were so mature because you were the first person in your class at school to grow a moustache.

Darren I was too — apart from Miss East, our history teacher.

Jane It wasn't till after we were married that I found out that you were a complete pillock.

Darren What!

Jane You're a wally, Darren.

Percival smiles

Darren How long after we got married did you think this?

Jane It was the second day of our honeymoon.

Percival It took you that long?

Jane It was then that I found out just how immature you really were.

Darren What did I do that was so bad?

Jane You dropped your trousers and mooned to everyone out of the train window.

Darren It was only a laugh.

Jane You were on the roundabout at Blackpool Pleasure Beach, for God's sake. There were women and kids everywhere.

Darren I was drunk.

Jane Yes. For the whole of our honeymoon. I knew then it was never going to get any better. I realized I had to change things for myself. So, over the years, I lost some weight, got my confidence back and enrolled myself in nightschool.

Darren You did?

Jane Yes. Believe it or not I can quite easily hold an intelligent conversation on almost any subject you care to mention.

Darren How come I've never heard any of this intelligent conversation then?

Percival It's almost too easy.

Darren (*to Percival*) Shut up you! (*He stands*)

Percival She could have a more intelligent conversation with a bowl of fruit.

Darren (*going to him*) I'm bloody well warning you, dodgey ticker or not.

Percival You do nothing to stimulate her, you fool.

Darren Don't you start going on about my sexual prowess.

Jane Shut up, Darren.

Darren (*moves to Jane*) You think you're so clever. Well, I could tell you something now that would devastate you.

Percival Yes. He used to wear a false moustache at school.

Darren (*going back to Percival*) I'm going to knock that smug grin off your face in a minute.

Percival (*getting up*) I feel it only fair to warn you I used to box for my regiment when I was younger. (*He stands behind the sofa*)

Darren And I feel it only fair to warn you I used to box for the checkouts at Tesco's. (*He joins Percival behind the sofa*)

Percival Oh well. Come on then. I'll give you the hiding of your life.

Darren Yeah? You and whose army?

Jane Sit down, Percival, before you give yourself a heart attack. And Darren, you can't even fight a cold, so stop it before you pull something.

Darren (*still squaring up*) I'm going to pull his head off and hit him in the face with it.

Percival I've killed bigger men than you to get to a fight.

He pushes Darren away

Darren Oh yeah?

Darren pushes Percival back even harder

Percival Yes.

Percival pushes Darren back harder still

Darren Yeah?

Darren pushes Percival back as hard as he can

Percival Yes.

Percival pushes Darren for all his worth. The men look at each other then walk towards each other like two gunfighters shouting "Yeah" and "Yes" until their noses are only an inch apart. Jane walks over to the sideboard and picks up the dinner gong which she bangs five or six times very loudly. The men stop and walk to their seats like two boxers at the end of a round

Jane That's better.

Percival picks up his glass of water and swills some around his mouth. Darren copies with a mouthful of damson wine. Percival sees that Darren is copying him so he swills twice more. Darren does the same. Percival gargles. Darren does the same. Percival puts his glass back on the table. So does Darren

Will you two stop behaving like kids?

Percival holds his hand up, walks over to Darren, picks up Darren's glass of wine and spits his mouthful of water into it. Then he puts the glass back on the table and returns, smiling, to his seat. Darren picks up his glass and peers into it

I don't believe this.

Darren puts his glass on the table and holds up his hand. He stands up. Percival quickly grabs his glass of water. Darren bends down and takes Percival's hat from under the table, spits his mouthful of wine into it, then throws the hat to Percival. Shouting triumphantly he sits

You're worse than infants.

Percival Did you see that? He just spat in my best hat!

Darren You're lucky my bladder was empty.

Jane If you two will stop I can continue. Now, where was I?

Percival You'd just got yourself an education. (*He puts his hat on the table*)

Jane Oh yes. It was then that I realized my job wasn't rewarding enough and I needed more of a challenge. So I resigned.

Darren You quit your job as an air hostess? You never told me! How long ago?

Jane Almost a year.

Percival Was it then that you started to work for the homeless?

Jane No, Percival. It wasn't.

Percival What did you do then?

Jane I started working for an escort agency.

Percival (*standing*) What! I can't believe it!

Darren (*also standing*) Neither can I! What do you know about selling cars?

Percival She's not selling cars, you moron!

Darren No?

Percival No. She's selling her body. She's on the game!

Jane (*loudly*) I most definitely am not!

Percival Well, what would you say your job is then?

Jane I escort business men to luncheons and parties when their wives can't attend.

Percival And then escort them to bed afterwards, no doubt. (*He sits*)

Jane I knew you would never understand.

Darren You never came to any parties with me. (*He sits on the sofa*)

Jane Maybe because you always ended up making a prat of yourself. A woman tends not to enjoy parties very much when her husband spends most of it being sick.

Darren That's not true.

Jane Do you know what all your friends call you?

Darren No.

Jane They call you "Darren the Bogbrush" because your head's always stuck down the toilet.

Darren You're making it up.

Percival So what exactly does your job entail?

Jane I've told you. Escorting business men to parties or to the races — anywhere they want to go with female company.

Percival Even to bed.

Jane No. Not to bed. I have to admit it does go on with some of the girls, but not with me. I just enjoy meeting normal, charming, witty people and getting paid for it.

Percival I've been to these so-called luncheons. I know what goes on at them.

Jane Of course you have, Percival. After all, we met at one, remember?

Percival (*remembering*) Oh my God. Yes!

Jane Yes, it was a delightful evening. And didn't I make good conversation.

Percival Yes. But I didn't know you were getting paid for it.

Jane Well, I must have made some sort of impression because you married me three months later.

Jane No wonder you didn't want a big society wedding. Not if you were married already.

Darren We did ours with the Co-op.

Percival Oh shut up, you.

Darren They know how to look after you at the Co-op.

Percival Stuff the bloody Co-op!

Darren You get interest-free credit. And stamps that help pay for your divorce. (*He thinks*) I suppose I'll have to cash them in now.

Percival Why the hell did you agree to marry me when you were already married to him?

Jane Because you were everything Darren wasn't. You were rich. Well educated. You had a powerful, important job. You were the exact opposite to him. (*She points to Darren*)

Percival You could have got a divorce. I'd have waited for you.

Jane No you wouldn't, Percival. You thought I was the unmarried daughter of a rich businessman. If you'd known my true circumstances you wouldn't have touched me with a barge-pole and you know it. So I thought I'd marry you and worry about divorcing Darren later.

Percival But how did you get the papers? A new birth certificate and everything?

Jane Oh that was easy. One of the girls at work goes out with a forger.

Percival So not only do you work with prostitutes, you're acquainted with the Underworld as well.

Jane Yes. Isn't it funny how our jobs run parallel?

Percival (*grabbing her hand*) If you were divorcing him, that means you must want me.

Jane No, Percival. I don't. (*She pulls her hand away*)

Percival (*standing*) But as you said, I'm rich, famous, well educated —

Jane Yes, yes, you are. But you're also the most big-headed, conceited, arrogant, pompous bore it's ever been my misfortune to meet, never mind marry.

Percival sits, shocked. Darren laughs loudly

Darren I don't know what most of that meant, but it sounded good.

Jane I had two goes at marriage with men from different ends of the social spectrum and I couldn't find happiness with either of you.

Percival But Amanda, what about the children?

Darren (*shocked*) You two got children?

Percival Bernice and Cecil from my first marriage. They think the world of her.

Jane Bernice is a spoilt seventeen year old schizophrenic bitch with a big attitude problem and an even bigger cocaine habit. And Cecil is so sexually hung up he can only get it together with a Mother Figure substitute and rubber clothing.

Percival You mean he's tried it on with you?

Jane Only every time I walked into the same room as him.

Percival I'm sorry. I didn't know.

Jane Of course you wouldn't. You were never at home. Anyway Cecil found out about my being married to Darren. He said no-one need know about it if we came to some agreement, which included my wearing a diving suit and spanking him with the flipper once a week. It was then that I decided the only course of action left open to me was to divorce you both and start my life again.

Percival But what are you going to do? Where are you going to stay?

Jane I'm moving into a flat with a friend.

Darren What friend?

Jane Tony is just a friend.

Percival Is he your lover?

Jane Yes, if you must know. Tony is my lover.

Percival (*standing*) Christ! You're married to two men, you've got a lover and you work part time for an escort agency.

Darren (*standing*) No wonder you didn't want that love-toy from the catalogue.

Jane (*turning on them*) Just shut up and sit down, the pair of you.

The men look at each other then sit again

I knew I had to tell you both. But I didn't think I'd be doing it at the same time. But in a way I'm glad I have. Now I've got nothing left to hide. I'm going upstairs to get my suitcases. Tony's going to be here in a few moments to pick me up.

She walks to the door

I really am sorry. I realize now everything was my fault. I should never have married either of you.

She goes out of the door and upstairs

Both men wait in silence for a while

Darren Well. What did you make of that?
Percival I only came here to buy a car.
Darren I still love her, you know.
Percival What?
Darren Your wife. I still love her.
Percival Yes. Well. So do I. But it doesn't make any difference now. She's leaving both of us.
Darren But what if there was only one of us?
Percival Sorry?
Darren If one of us was to accept the divorce and leave the other free to try and patch things up.
Percival Aren't you forgetting something?
Darren What?
Percival This new man, Tony.
Darren Well, I'm prepared to fight for her even if you're not.
Percival Of course I am, but how are we going to decide which one leaves.
Darren I don't know.
Percival I could possibly offer you a very large sum of money.
Darren (*standing*) And I could possibly give you a very large punch on the nose. How dare you try and buy me off? Your sort think money can get you anything. (*He sits*) Exactly how much was you thinking of?
Percival As much as it takes.
Darren (*stopping himself*) No. It doesn't matter. My marriage means more to me than money.
Percival Well, how are we going to decide?
Darren I don't know.

Both men think

Do you play poker?
Percival We haven't got time, have we? Tony's on his way to pick her up.

Darren I know. We'll toss a coin.
Percival No. That relies too much on luck.
Darren What then?
Percival Do you play spoof?
Darren (*smiling*) Do I play spoof?

They stand face to face

   You call first.

Percival puts his hand in his pocket. Darren doesn't have pockets — he takes his money from the "Mickey Mouse" purse hanging round his neck. Percival tries to sneak a look. Darren sees him and turns his back on him. Then they both hold out their hands

Percival thinks

Percival Five.

Darren thinks

Darren Four.

Both men open their hands and count the coins. Percival has two. Darren has one

Percival Damn.
Darren Sod it.
Percival Right. Your call.

They have another go

Darren Right. Right. Let me think. I want a good 'un. Come on. Come on.
Percival Just stick your hand out and forget the running commentary.

   Jane comes into the room, carrying a case

The men are too engrossed to notice. She walks over to them

Darren (*tapping his foot*) Right — right — come on — think — think.
Percival Hurry up. Take a guess, man.

Jane puts her case down

Darren All right. All right. (*He shuts his eyes to concentrate, then shouts*) Three!
Percival Three. Ah. (*He is nervous too*) Bad call, bad call.
Darren I've got it on the button. I know I have.
Percival I'll say — one!

Jane puts her hand between theirs. Only then do they see her

Jane Spoof!

Both men look at her. Darren opens his hand — he has nothing. Percival opens his — he has nothing too. They look at Jane. She slowly opens her hand to reveal nothing

  I win!
Percival Best of three!

Jane looks at them

Jane Yes, I probably am. Now I'd like a quick word in private with each of you, starting with you, Darren.

She points at Darren. He sits on the sofa

Percival Why him?
Jane Because I married him first, that's why.
Percival As good a reason as any, I suppose. Where shall I wait?
Jane In the kitchen.
Percival I don't even go into the kitchen in my own house.

Jane I know.

Percival slowly walks out to the kitchen

Now, Darren —— (*She fetches her bag from the cabinet and then moves* DSL)

Darren I've got a confession to make to you, Jane.

Jane You have?

Darren Yes. You're not the only one that's been living a double life, you know. (*He moves to Jane*)

Jane I'm not?

Darren Oh no. I didn't really want to tell you this but here goes. For the last year I've been having a passionate affair with the young widow next door.

Jane (*looking up*) Mrs Peters!

Darren Yes. You're shocked, ain't you?

Jane Not really. I knew all about it. In fact it was my idea. (*She walks away to behind the armchair*)

Darren What! (*He moves after her*)

Jane About a year ago she told me she quite fancied you and I said I didn't mind.

Darren You don't know the best bit yet. Last summer when you were working we had a two week holiday together.

Jane Yes, I know. I paid for it.

Darren (*open-mouthed*) What!

Jane I said "I know. I paid for it".

Darren You're lying!

Jane You had a two week holiday in Spain that coincided with Wimbledon fortnight.

Darren What's Wimbledon got to do with it?

Jane While you and Mrs Peters were in Spain, I brought two Arab families over to England to watch the whole of Wimbledon. They stayed in this house and Mrs Peter's the whole fortnight. Your holiday cost nothing compared to what I made from the agency.

Darren is completely stunned

Game, set and match to me, I think.

He sits slowly

Now I want to talk to you about my divorce settlement.
Darren I'm not paying you a penny!
Jane That's just it. I don't want anything from you.
Darren You don't?
Jane No — unless you tell anyone what's happened here today, of
course.
Darren You're buying my silence?
Jane Yes. If you open your mouth about this I'll be back and I'll take
everything. The house, the bank balance and whatever else my
lawyers can squeeze out of you. Do I make myself clear?
Darren Perfectly.

Jane takes a powder compact from her bag

Jane Good. Now, if you could just swap places with Percival in the
kitchen ...

Darren slowly stands then walks towards the kitchen. He turns.
Jane is applying powder to her nose

Darren I'll never be able to go on stage again. You've destroyed
all my confidence.
Jane You only got bookings because you were a crap Elvis
impersonator anyway.
Darren What?
Jane You're rubbish, Darren, that's why people book you. So they
can have a good laugh.
Darren What about my "Old Shep"? There was never a dry eye in
the place when I finished with that.
Jane Only because the punters were wetting themselves laughing.
Darren You're lying!
Jane They say "Old Shep" used to hear you singing and throw

himself on the vet's needle. (*She sees that she has hurt him*) I'm
sorry, Darren, but it's the truth.
Darren I never knew. (*He slowly sits down on the sofa*) All this time
and I never knew.
Jane (*putting her hand on his shoulder*) I know — and that was the
saddest part of your whole act.

*He shrugs her hand from his shoulder and goes to the kitchen. Jane
goes to her bag and is applying perfume as ——*

Percival comes in

Percival What's the matter with him?
Jane I think "Old Shep's" come back to haunt him.
Percival Your car never was written off, was it? That is the same
car standing outside?
Jane Yes. (*She takes a brush from her bag*)
Percival But why?
Jane We needed a car and you had so many. (*She brushes her hair*)
Percival How did you manage to keep up this charade for so long?
Jane It wasn't easy and I'm glad it's over. Now I want to talk about
my divorce settlement. (*She puts the brush away*)
Percival I'm not paying you a penny! (*He sits on the sofa*)
Jane I'm afraid you're going to have to, Percival. I need to pay half
on Tony's flat.
Percival I'll see you in hell first.
Jane Undoubtedly. But I need somewhere to live till then.
Percival I'm not paying for you and your lover's den of iniquity.
Jane I was hoping you wouldn't take this attitude.
Percival Oh, and what attitude did you think I'd take, for God's
sake?
Jane I could get more than the money I need if I take my story to
the papers.
Percival You charlatan!
Jane I don't want to. I just want to melt away and you'd never see
me again.

Percival It wouldn't be the end of the world if the papers found out.
I could survive it. Anyway you seem to have overlooked one very
important factor.
Jane Oh? What's that?

Percival stands and moves to her

Percival Polyandry is a criminal offence. If you blab to the tabloids
you could be facing up to five years in prison.
Jane I thought you'd be pig-headed enough to try and bluff it out,
so I did some research into your family history. Your name's not
Hitchcock at all. It's Kwaitkowski and your grandfather bought
your title for fifty pounds in 1943 when he came to England from
Poland.
Percival (*slightly unnerved*) It's not a great secret. It's there for
anyone to see if they look in the right books.
Jane Yes. But what isn't quite so clear is why your family left
Poland in the first place.
Percival (*even more unnerved*) They left to escape Nazi repression
of course.
Jane That's not quite true, is it? Your family were collaborators and
they fled Poland before the end of the war with all their ill-gotten
gains before their own people could shoot them.

Percival stands silent. Jane takes an envelope from her bag

You'll find the sum of money I need isn't extortionate and you'll
be able to claim it back in a year or so on expenses. (*She gives
Percival the envelope*) Now, if you'll just get Darren in from the
kitchen, I'd like to say goodbye to you both together.

Percival slowly turns and walks out to the kitchen

*A car horn sounds offstage. Jane runs to the window and beckons
someone to come in. She puts her case on the armchair as ——*

Darren and Percival walk in from the kitchen

Darren You've trussed us up like a couple of old turkeys. (*He sits on the sofa*)

Jane It's for the best, believe me. It will be less painful for everyone this way.

The doorbell rings

Excuse me.

She goes out to answer it

Percival She conned me into marriage, used her position to exploit whatever she wanted, extorted money out of me on false pretences and now she's blackmailing me. (*He thinks*) What a woman! We could do with her in parliament. (*He sits next to Darren on the sofa*)

Jane returns

Jane Darren, Percival — I'd like you to meet Tony.

A pretty woman walks through from the hall

Percival Oh my God!
Darren I don't believe it! It's a woman!
Percival (*turning to Darren*) I see you graduated in biology then?
Darren You mean they're a couple of dykes!
Jane Yes, Darren. We are. (*She takes Tony's hand*) It was after I met Tony I knew I'd have to divorce you both. (*She turns to Tony*) Could you take my case to the car, darling? I'll be with you in a moment. (*She pecks Tony on the cheek*)

Tony walks to the case. Darren goes to grab the handle but Tony slaps his hand away. Shocked and stunned he backs away, nursing his hand. Tony picks up the case and walks to the door. Before going out, she stops, puts down the case, turns and looks at the men, then walks over to Jane. The women embrace in a passionate kiss

Darren I think I'm going to throw up. (*He sits on Percival's coat on the sofa*)
Percival I think I'll join you.

The women finish kissing

Tony again looks at both men, turns and walks out with the case

Jane I know this must be a shock to you both.
Percival Not ever one for understatements, are we?
Jane Just think how much more embarrassing it would be for you, Percival, if the papers got hold of this. And you, Darren, what kind of man would your friends think you are? To know your wife ran off with another woman?

Silence. She picks up her coat and bag from the chair

Well, I don't suppose I'll see either of you again, so — be lucky, won't you.

She goes out through the hall doorway and the front door slams shut

Silence for a long while. Percival slowly walks over to the table, picks up his hat, goes to put it on but stops. It still has water in it, so he doesn't bother. He sighs and sits on the sofa next to Darren. Another long silence

Darren (*eventually*) Well?
Percival (*not looking at him*) Well what?
Darren (*pause*) Do you want the car or not?
Percival (*pause*) I don't know.
Darren (*pause*) It's only had "One Careful Owner".

They slowly turn and look at each other as the Curtain *closes*

FURNITURE AND PROPERTY LIST

Further dressing may be added at the director's discretion

On stage: Cottage-style sofa. *On it*: empty crisp packets, old newspapers, sweet wrappings, blackened banana skin
Armchair. *On it*: pile of washing
Coffee table. *On it*: framed wedding photo
Cabinet. *On it*: bottle of whisky, three glasses, dinner gong and beater
Plant stand. *In it*: plant

Off stage: Two mugs of coffee (**Darren**)
Guitar (**Darren**)
Handbag. *In it*: powder compact, perfume, envelope, brush (**Jane**)
Glass of water (**Darren**)
Case (**Jane**)

Personal: **Percival**: wrist-watch (used throughout), tablets, coins
Darren: "Mickey Mouse" purse. *In it*: coins

LIGHTING PLOT

Property fittings required: nil
Interior. The same throughout

To open: Overall general lighting

No cues

EFFECTS PLOT